Earthforms

Oceans

by Kay Jackson

Consultant:
John D. Vitek
Assistant Dean of Graduate Studies
Texas A & M University
College Station, Texas

Capstone *press*

Mankato, Minnesota

Bridgestone Books are published by Capstone Press,
151 Good Counsel Drive, P.O. Box 669, Mankato, Minnesota 56002.
www.capstonepress.com

Library of Congress Cataloging-in-Publication Data
Jackson, Kay, 1959–
    Oceans / Kay Jackson.
    p. cm.—(Bridgestone books. Earthforms)
    Summary: "Describes oceans, including how they formed, ocean plants and animals, how people
and weather change oceans, the Atlantic Ocean, and the Pacific Ocean"—Provided by publisher.
    Includes bibliographical references and index.
    ISBN-13: 978-0-7368-5406-1 (hardcover)
    ISBN-10: 0-7368-5406-1 (hardcover)
    1. Ocean—Juvenile literature. I. Title. II. Bridgestone Books. Earthforms.
GC21.5J33 2006
  551.46—dc22   2005015248

Editorial Credits

Becky Viaene, editor; Juliette Peters, set designer; Patrick D. Dentinger, book designer;
    Anne P. McMullen, illustrator; Jo Miller, photo researcher; Scott Thoms, photo editor

Photo Credits

Corbis/Bettmann, 14; Martin Harvey, cover
Digital Vision, 10
The Image Finders, Mark E. Gibson, 16
Peter Arnold, Inc./Weatherstock, 12
Seapics.com/Doug Perrine 18; James D. Watt, 4; Phillip Colla, 8
Visuals Unlimited/Reinhard Dirscherl, 1

1 2 3 4 5 6 11 10 09 08 07 06

Table of Contents

What Are Oceans?

Oceans are huge bodies of salt water. All earth's ocean water is connected and called the World Ocean. This huge ocean is divided by the **continents** into five main areas. These areas are named Arctic, Atlantic, Indian, Pacific, and Southern.

Ocean water is constantly moving between these five areas. Wind causes **currents** that move water across an ocean. **Tides**, caused by pulling of the earth's moon and sun, lower and raise the water level.

◄ A surfer looks out at the Pacific Ocean, and gets ready to brave the waves.

How Did Oceans Form?

Long ago, earth was very hot. Volcanoes shot **water vapor** and other gases into the air. Over time, clouds formed and rain fell. After millions of years, rain filled low spots in the earth's crust. The water in these low spots became the oceans.

Oceans slowly became salty. Rivers washed salt from the land into the oceans. Today, 1 gallon (3.8 liters) of ocean water holds about 1 cup (0.2 liters) of salt.

◀ A long time ago, gases from volcanoes formed clouds. Rain from clouds fell and became the oceans.

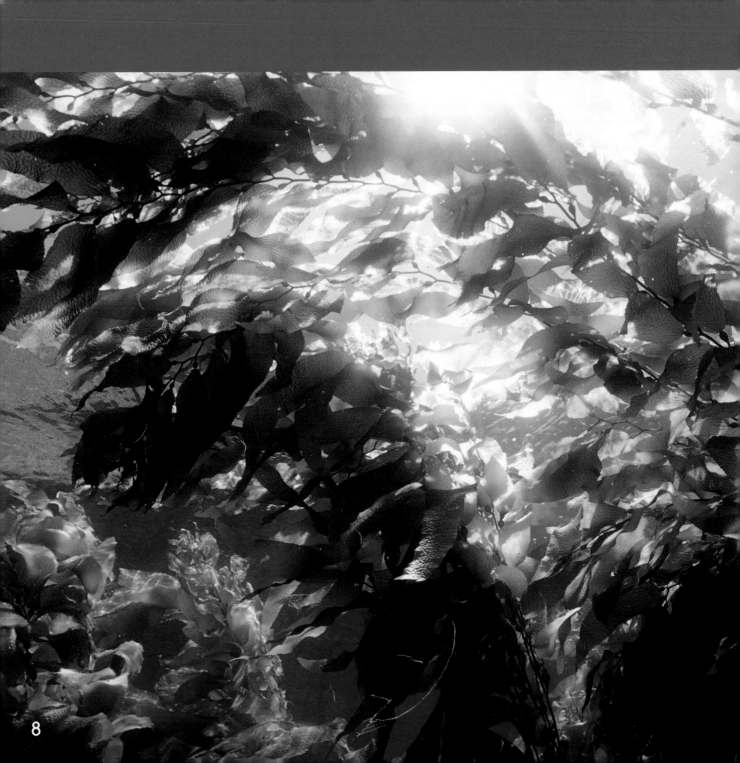

Ocean Plants

Almost all ocean plants grow near the water's surface. Ranging from large to small, **algae** are the most common ocean plants. Some tiny algae can only be seen with a microscope. Large algae, called giant kelp, can grow to be 100 feet (30 meters) tall.

Few ocean plants are able to grow below 660 feet (200 meters). Here, little sunlight reaches the plants. Deeper down, no plants grow in the dark ocean water.

◄ Thick forests of giant kelp may grow 2 feet (24 inches) in a single day.

Ocean Animals

Like plants, most ocean animals live only in sunny water. **Zooplankton** live in this sunlit zone. Fish, including giant sharks, eat these tiny animals. Other ocean animals, such as dolphins and jellyfish, also eat zooplankton.

The anglerfish, giant squid, and other unique animals live deep in the dark oceans. Anglerfish have a rod between their eyes. The rod's tip glows and attracts curious fish. If a fish swims too close, the anglerfish grabs it.

◄ Near coral reefs, hundreds of brightly colored fish swim in the warm ocean water.

Weather Changes Oceans

Powerful storms called hurricanes can change an ocean's **coastline**. Hurricanes form over the ocean and push large waves onto land. Waves can move sand from beaches into the ocean.

Long periods of warm or cold weather can change an ocean's water level. Warm weather melts large amounts of ice at the North and South Poles. Melting ice raises the water level and covers land. Cold weather lowers the water level by freezing more water back into ice at the poles.

◄ Strong winds from Hurricane George push waves onto the south coast of Florida.

People Change Oceans

People change oceans by **polluting** the water. Some factories dump chemicals into oceans. Huge ships sometimes spill oil and garbage into the water.

People also change ocean life. For years, fishers have caught nets full of crab, tuna, and shrimp. Overfishing has left bluefin tuna and other fish **endangered**.

Some countries want to protect ocean animals and plants. They have passed laws to keep oceans clean.

◄ A broken oil well spills millions of gallons of oil into the Atlantic Ocean.

The Pacific Ocean

The Pacific is the largest and deepest part of the World Ocean. Asia and Australia lie on the west side. North and South America are on the east. The Pacific's Mariana Trench is the deepest part of the ocean. It is almost 7 miles (11 kilometers) deep.

Every day, ships cross the deep Pacific. Factories send products like TVs, bicycles, and shoes worldwide on these ships.

Whales also move through the Pacific. Each year, blue whales travel across thousands of miles of ocean.

◄ Large ships move products across the Pacific Ocean.

The Atlantic Ocean

Separated from the Pacific by North and South America, the Atlantic Ocean is also huge. It is the second largest part of the World Ocean. The Atlantic Ocean divides the Eastern and Western Hemispheres.

In warm Atlantic waters, coral reefs are home to thousands of animals. Parrotfish scrape algae off rocks. Damselfish swim between fan corals.

In the cold northern Atlantic, polar bears hunt seals. Hammerhead sharks swim quickly through the water. Walruses eat clams.

◀ A colorful stoplight parrotfish swims through a coral reef in the Atlantic Ocean.

EARTH'S OCEANS

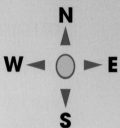

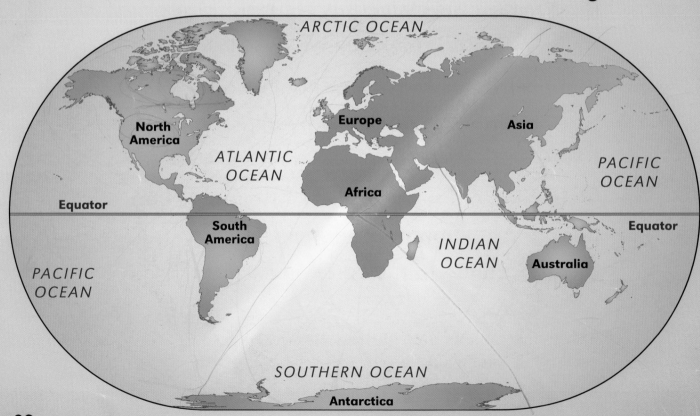

ARCTIC OCEAN

North America

Europe

Asia

ATLANTIC OCEAN

PACIFIC OCEAN

Africa

Equator

Equator

South America

INDIAN OCEAN

Australia

PACIFIC OCEAN

SOUTHERN OCEAN

Antarctica

Oceans on a Map

People use different types of maps to learn about oceans. On colored maps, blue shows ocean water and how it connects as the World Ocean. Some maps show how ocean currents flow. Other maps show what the ocean floor looks like.

Because oceans cover so much of the world, their health is important. Oceans are home to thousands of plants and animals. Ocean plants make much of the oxygen that people and animals breathe. The health of oceans will continue to be important.

◀ Oceans cover two-thirds of the earth. The continents separate the World Ocean into five areas.

Glossary

algae (AL-jee)—small plants without roots or stems that grow in water or on damp surfaces

coastline (KOHST-line)—the place where land and ocean meet

continent (KON-tuh-nuhnt)—one of the seven main landmasses of earth

current (KUR-uhnt)—the movement of water in a river or an ocean

endangered (en-DAYN-jurd)—at risk of dying out

pollute (puh-LOOT)—to make something dirty or unsafe

tide (TIDE)—the constant change in sea level that is caused by the pull of the moon and the sun on earth

water vapor (WAH-tur VAY-pur)—water in the form of a gas

zooplankton (zoo-PLANGK-tuhn)—tiny animals that drift in the water

Read More

Dell, Pamela. *Ocean Plants.* Life in the World's Biomes. Mankato, Minn.: Capstone Press, 2006.

Royston, Angela. *Oceans.* My World of Geography. Chicago: Heinemann Library, 2005.

Internet Sites

FactHound offers a safe, fun way to find Internet sites related to this book. All of the sites on FactHound have been researched by our staff.

Here's how:
1. Visit *www.facthound.com*
2. Type in this special code **0736854061** for age-appropriate sites. Or enter a search word related to this book for a more general search.
3. Click on the **Fetch It** button.

FactHound will fetch the best sites for you!

Index